Easy Listening Practice for the New TOEIC® L&R Test

やさしいTOEIC® L&Rテスト

リスニングパート攻略

Tyler Burden
Tsuyoshi Chiba
Yau-Sin Cheng
Kiyoshi Fukasawa
Takamasa Fukuoka
Satomi Washiya

JN003130

NAN'UN-DO

Download Audio

音声ファイル
無料 DL
のご案内

このテキストの音声を無料で視聴（ストリーミング）・ダウンロードできます。自習用音声としてご活用ください。
以下のサイトにアクセスしてテキスト番号で検索してください。

https://nanun-do.com　テキスト番号［ **512231** ］

※ 無線 LAN（WiFi）に接続してのご利用を推奨いたします。

※ 音声ダウンロードは Zip ファイルでの提供になります。
お使いの機器によっては別途ソフトウェア（アプリケーション）の導入が必要となります。

※ Easy Listening Practice for the New TOEIC® L&R Test
音声ダウンロードページは以下の QR コードからもご利用になれます。

Read by

Chris Koprowski（米）
Guy Perryman（英）
Shizuka Anderson（加）
Sarah Greaves（豪）

Easy Listening Practice for the New TOEIC® L&R Test

© Copyright 2024
by
Tyler Burden
Tsuyoshi Chiba
Yau-Sin Cheng
Kiyoshi Fukasawa
Takamasa Fukuoka
Satomi Washiya

All rights Reserved
No part of this book may be reproduced in any form without
permission from the authors and Nan'un-do Co., Ltd.

TOEIC is a registered trademark of Educational Testing Service (ETS).
This publication is not endorsed or approved by ETS.

TOEIC® Listening & Reading Test について

TOEIC® (Test of English for International Communication) とは、アメリカのテスト専門機関 ETS（Educational Testing Service）が開発及び製作した、国際的コミュニケーション能力を測定するテストの総称です。中でも TOEIC® Listening & Reading Test は、英語力を測定するテストとして、日本の多くの企業で採用や昇進などの際に活用されています。

1. テスト形式と特徴

リスニングとリーディングの能力を測定するマークシート方式の一斉客観テストで、以下の特徴があります。

- テストは全て英文。日本語は一切使われない。
- 英文和訳や和文英訳などの設問は出題されない。
- 日常及びビジネスのコミュニケーション場面を想定した問題設定。
- アメリカ・イギリスだけでなく、カナダ・オーストラリア・ニュージーランドの発音も採用。

2. 試験時間と問題数

リスニングの試験時間は約 45 分で 100 問、リーディングの試験時間は 75 分で出題数は 100 問、合計、出題数が 200 問の約 2 時間のテストです。

3. テストの結果

テスト結果は、990 点を満点とするスコアで評価されます。リスニングとリーディング、どちらもそれぞれ 5 ～ 495 点の範囲で 5 点刻みで評価します。

本書の構成

本書の Part 1 から Part 4 の問題は、TOEIC® Listening & Reading Test のリスニングセクションで出題される質問形式に基づいて作成されています。

Before Listening

各ユニットに出てくるキーワードやフレーズを学びます。次のリスニングの内容が理解できるように配慮されています。リスニングを向上させるというよりも基礎的な英語表現を学習します。

Part 1 Photograph

写真を見ながらリスニング問題の正解を選択します。

Part 2 Question-Response

各ユニットのテーマに沿ったリスニング問題です。併せて基本的な英会話表現も学習します。発話に対する最適な応答を選びましょう。

Part 3 Conversation

男女の短い会話をリスニングした後で、その会話の内容についての選択問題です。

Part 4 Talk

短いストーリーをリスニングした後で、その内容についての選択問題です。内容をよく把握した上で解答を選択しましょう。

Contents

Unit 1 In Flight 機内にて

Before Listening　Mini Vocabulary Quiz

Choose the correct meaning.

1. row
   (A) a small man　(B) not cooked　(C) rule　(D) a line of seats
2. conference
   (A) official meeting　(B) festival　(C) fight　(D) radio signals
3. on board
   (A) on sale　(B) in the woods　(C) on a plane　(D) in the field
4. altitude
   (A) the weight　(B) the width　(C) the bottom　(D) the height
5. sit back
   (A) feel comfortable　(B) be worried　(C) get sick　(D) get back home

Part 1 Photograph

02

Ⓐ Ⓑ Ⓒ Ⓓ

Part 2 Question-Response

03

1. Mark your answer.　Ⓐ Ⓑ Ⓒ
2. Mark your answer.　Ⓐ Ⓑ Ⓒ
3. Mark your answer.　Ⓐ Ⓑ Ⓒ

Part 3 Conversation

04

1. Where are the people going?
   (A) The UK
   (B) The US
   (C) Japan
   (D) The UAE

   Ⓐ Ⓑ Ⓒ Ⓓ

2. What's the purpose of the man's visit?
   (A) It's a vacation.
   (B) He's going home.
   (C) He's visiting members of his family.
   (D) He's going to a conference.

   Ⓐ Ⓑ Ⓒ Ⓓ

3. What's the woman's job?
   (A) She's a professor.
   (B) She's a businesswoman.
   (C) She doesn't have a job.
   (D) She's a musician.

   Ⓐ Ⓑ Ⓒ Ⓓ

Part 4 Talk

05

1. Who is speaking?
   (A) A passenger
   (B) A flight attendant
   (C) A soldier
   (D) A pilot

   Ⓐ Ⓑ Ⓒ Ⓓ

2. Where are they flying?
   (A) Within Asia
   (B) Within Europe
   (C) Within North America
   (D) Within Africa

   Ⓐ Ⓑ Ⓒ Ⓓ

3. What time will they land?
   (A) 2:00
   (B) 2:20
   (C) 3:00
   (D) 3:30

   Ⓐ Ⓑ Ⓒ Ⓓ

Unit 2 Check in ホテル・チェックイン

Before Listening Grammar check

Which sentence is correct?

1. (A) Breakfast is served from 6 to 9.
   (B) Breakfast is serving from 6 to 9.

2. (A) Your room is 327 when is on the third floor.
   (B) Your room is 327 which is on the third floor.

3. (A) You can contact reception by dialing "0."
   (B) You can contact reception to dial "0."

Part 1 Photograph

06

Ⓐ Ⓑ Ⓒ Ⓓ

Part 2 Question-Response

07

1. Mark your answer. Ⓐ Ⓑ Ⓒ
2. Mark your answer. Ⓐ Ⓑ Ⓒ
3. Mark your answer. Ⓐ Ⓑ Ⓒ

Part 3 Conversation

08

1. Where is the conversation taking place?
   (A) At the reception
   (B) Over the phone
   (C) In the dining room
   (D) In the guest's bedroom

   Ⓐ Ⓑ Ⓒ Ⓓ

2. How many nights is the guest staying at the hotel?
   (A) 1
   (B) 2
   (C) 3
   (D) 4

   Ⓐ Ⓑ Ⓒ Ⓓ

3. What can the guest see from his room?
   (A) The sea
   (B) The city
   (C) Mountains
   (D) A garden

   Ⓐ Ⓑ Ⓒ Ⓓ

Part 4 Talk

09

1. Who is speaking?
   (A) A hotel guest
   (B) A hotel chef
   (C) A hotel receptionist
   (D) A hotel porter

   Ⓐ Ⓑ Ⓒ Ⓓ

2. Where is the dining room?
   (A) On the 1st floor
   (B) On the 2nd floor
   (C) On the 3rd floor
   (D) Next to the reception desk

   Ⓐ Ⓑ Ⓒ Ⓓ

3. What must the guest do to get breakfast?
   (A) Pay some extra money
   (B) Show a key card
   (C) Give the staff a voucher
   (D) Walk to a nearby restaurant

   Ⓐ Ⓑ Ⓒ Ⓓ

Unit 3 On the Underground 地下鉄にて

Before Listening

Fill in the blanks with the correct words.

1. May I have your attention (　　) platform 1?
2. The train has been delayed due (　　) an accident.
3. Get off the train (　　) Oxford Street.
4. We apologize (　　) the inconvenience.

(A) to	(B) on	(C) for	(D) at

Part 1 Photograph

10

Ⓐ Ⓑ Ⓒ Ⓓ

Part 2 Question-Response

11

1. Mark your answer. Ⓐ Ⓑ Ⓒ
2. Mark your answer. Ⓐ Ⓑ Ⓒ
3. Mark your answer. Ⓐ Ⓑ Ⓒ

Part 3 Conversation

12

1. Where is the man going?
   (A) To the center of the city
   (B) To the airport
   (C) For a walk in the countryside
   (D) To a shop to buy oysters
   Ⓐ Ⓑ Ⓒ Ⓓ

2. What's the best way to travel?
   (A) By bus
   (B) By taxi
   (C) By underground train
   (D) By regular train
   Ⓐ Ⓑ Ⓒ Ⓓ

3. What's the woman's advice?
   (A) To visit Oxford Street
   (B) To buy a discount card
   (C) To avoid central London
   (D) To buy a good pair of shoes
   Ⓐ Ⓑ Ⓒ Ⓓ

Part 4 Talk

13

1. On which train line is there a problem?
   (A) The District Line
   (B) The Piccadilly Line
   (C) The Circle Line
   (D) The Bakerloo Line
   Ⓐ Ⓑ Ⓒ Ⓓ

2. What is the problem?
   (A) The train is too crowded.
   (B) The train is going to be late.
   (C) The train has been cancelled.
   (D) The fire alarm is ringing.
   Ⓐ Ⓑ Ⓒ Ⓓ

3. What should passengers do?
   (A) Wait until the problem has been solved
   (B) Take a train on a different line
   (C) Take a bus
   (D) Leave the station immediately
   Ⓐ Ⓑ Ⓒ Ⓓ

Unit 4 Smartphones スマホ

Before Listening

Fill in the blanks with the correct words.

1. I can't find (　　) the smartphone is.
   (A) where　(B) when　(C) that
2. She doesn't know (　　) to adjust her smartphone.
   (A) but　(B) that　(C) how
3. Even (　　) you drop it, it won't break.
   (A) and　(B) if　(C) what
4. Best of (　　), the smartphone costs only 80 dollars.
   (A) all　(B) every　(C) only

Part 1 Photograph

14

Ⓐ Ⓑ Ⓒ Ⓓ

Part 2 Question-Response

15

1. Mark your answer.　Ⓐ Ⓑ Ⓒ
2. Mark your answer.　Ⓐ Ⓑ Ⓒ
3. Mark your answer.　Ⓐ Ⓑ Ⓒ

Part 3 Conversation

16

1. What has the woman bought recently?
   (A) A computer
   (B) Speakers
   (C) A smartphone
   (D) A musical instrument

   Ⓐ Ⓑ Ⓒ Ⓓ

2. What's the problem?
   (A) Her smartphone is broken.
   (B) She doesn't like her smartphone.
   (C) She doesn't know how to switch her smartphone off.
   (D) She doesn't know how to adjust her smartphone.

   Ⓐ Ⓑ Ⓒ Ⓓ

3. What will the woman do next?
   (A) Buy a new smartphone
   (B) Get her smartphone repaired
   (C) Go back to the shop
   (D) Go online to get information

   Ⓐ Ⓑ Ⓒ Ⓓ

Part 4 Talk

17

1. Who is talking?
   (A) A customer
   (B) A salesperson
   (C) A doctor
   (D) A student

   Ⓐ Ⓑ Ⓒ Ⓓ

2. How much does the smartphone cost?
   (A) 16 pounds
   (B) 540 pounds
   (C) 850 pounds
   (D) 12,000 pounds

   Ⓐ Ⓑ Ⓒ Ⓓ

3. Which of the following sentences is true of the smartphone?
   (A) It will break if it gets wet.
   (B) It can't record videos.
   (C) There is a choice of colors.
   (D) Customers can buy a blue one.

   Ⓐ Ⓑ Ⓒ Ⓓ

Unit 5 The Internet インターネット

Before Listening Grammar check

Which sentence is correct?

1. (A) I can't stop him playing games.
   (B) I can't stop him to playing games.
2. (A) If the answer will be yes, it was a problem.
   (B) If the answer is yes, it's a problem.
3. (A) This novel is as better as that novel.
   (B) This novel is as bad as that novel.

Part 1 Photograph

18

Ⓐ Ⓑ Ⓒ Ⓓ

Part 2 Question-Response

19

1. Mark your answer. Ⓐ Ⓑ Ⓒ
2. Mark your answer. Ⓐ Ⓑ Ⓒ
3. Mark your answer. Ⓐ Ⓑ Ⓒ

Part 3 Conversation

20

1. Who is speaking?
   (A) A taxi driver and customer
   (B) A teacher and student
   (C) A computer programmer and boss
   (D) A hotel receptionist and guest
   Ⓐ Ⓑ Ⓒ Ⓓ

2. What does the woman want to do?
   (A) Reset her password
   (B) Use the Internet
   (C) Reserve a room
   (D) Visit the capital city
   Ⓐ Ⓑ Ⓒ Ⓓ

3. What is the correct password?
   (A) hotelsun304
   (B) HotelSun304
   (C) hotelsun314
   (D) HotelSun314
   Ⓐ Ⓑ Ⓒ Ⓓ

Part 4 Talk

21

1. Who is the message for?
   (A) Children
   (B) Teachers
   (C) Parents
   (D) Doctors
   Ⓐ Ⓑ Ⓒ Ⓓ

2. What is the problem?
   (A) Drug addiction
   (B) Internet addiction
   (C) Computer viruses
   (D) Alcohol addiction
   Ⓐ Ⓑ Ⓒ Ⓓ

3. What should a person do to get help?
   (A) Call a telephone number
   (B) Visit a website
   (C) Go to the hospital
   (D) Talk to a teacher
   Ⓐ Ⓑ Ⓒ Ⓓ

Unit 6 Campus Life キャンパスライフ

Before Listening Vocabulary Match

Match the words.

1. assignment (A) language rules
2. examination (B) test
3. grammar (C) task
4. semester (D) term

Part 1 Photograph

22

Ⓐ Ⓑ Ⓒ Ⓓ

Part 2 Question-Response

23

1. Mark your answer. Ⓐ Ⓑ Ⓒ
2. Mark your answer. Ⓐ Ⓑ Ⓒ
3. Mark your answer. Ⓐ Ⓑ Ⓒ

Part 3 Conversation

24

1. Where is the woman going first?
   (A) The classroom
   (B) The library
   (C) Home
   (D) The cafeteria
   Ⓐ Ⓑ Ⓒ Ⓓ

2. What language is the man studying?
   (A) Japanese
   (B) English
   (C) Chinese
   (D) French
   Ⓐ Ⓑ Ⓒ Ⓓ

3. When will they meet again?
   (A) In the first period class
   (B) In the second period class
   (C) At lunchtime
   (D) After lunch
   Ⓐ Ⓑ Ⓒ Ⓓ

Part 4 Talk

25

1. Who is talking?
   (A) A student
   (B) A teacher
   (C) A parent
   (D) A librarian
   Ⓐ Ⓑ Ⓒ Ⓓ

2. What language will the presentation be given in?
   (A) Japanese
   (B) Korean
   (C) Chinese
   (D) English
   Ⓐ Ⓑ Ⓒ Ⓓ

3. What score do students need for their homework assignments to pass the course?
   (A) An average of 60 percent
   (B) An average of 70 percent
   (C) An average of 80 percent
   (D) There are no homework assignments.
   Ⓐ Ⓑ Ⓒ Ⓓ

Unit 7 Tennis Tournament テニストーナメント

Before Listening Grammar check

Which sentence is correct?

1. (A) I think he will win the tournament.
   (B) I thought he will win the tournament.
2. (A) The last tennis match was tired.
   (B) The last tennis match was tiring.
3. (A) He has won the game twice.
   (B) He has won the game last year.

Part 1 Photograph

26

Ⓐ Ⓑ Ⓒ Ⓓ

Part 2 Question-Response

27

1. Mark your answer. Ⓐ Ⓑ Ⓒ
2. Mark your answer. Ⓐ Ⓑ Ⓒ
3. Mark your answer. Ⓐ Ⓑ Ⓒ

Part 3 Conversation

28

1. What tennis tournament are they talking about?
   (A) Wimbledon
   (B) The French Open
   (C) The US Open
   (D) The Australian Open

   Ⓐ Ⓑ Ⓒ Ⓓ

2. What match are they talking about?
   (A) A first-round match
   (B) A quarter-final match
   (C) A semi-final match
   (D) The final match

   Ⓐ Ⓑ Ⓒ Ⓓ

3. Why does the man think Andy Ward will win?
   (A) Because he usually beats Stefanos Adell
   (B) Because he has a better serve
   (C) Because Stefanos Adell's last match was tiring
   (D) Because he is faster than Stefanos Adell

   Ⓐ Ⓑ Ⓒ Ⓓ

Part 4 Talk

29

1. Who is talking?
   (A) A tennis player
   (B) A tennis coach
   (C) A journalist
   (D) A tournament organizer

   Ⓐ Ⓑ Ⓒ Ⓓ

2. Why is the speaker retiring?
   (A) Because he's old
   (B) Because he wants to do other things
   (C) Because he cannot play well any more
   (D) Because he wants to retire while he is the number one player in the world

   Ⓐ Ⓑ Ⓒ Ⓓ

3. Which is true about the speaker?
   (A) He has never won the US Open.
   (B) He has never been injured.
   (C) He has had a successful career.
   (D) This is her first tournament in the US.

   Ⓐ Ⓑ Ⓒ Ⓓ

Unit 8 Music: Beatles Festival ビートルズ祭り

Before Listening

Fill in the blanks with correct words.

1. There were a lot of people in the venue.
   = The venue was (   ) of people.
2. There are tickets available for April 1st.
   = We (   ) have the tickets for April 1st.
3. A lot of people watched the show.
   = There were (   ) viewers of the show.

Part 1 Photograph

30

Ⓐ Ⓑ Ⓒ Ⓓ

Part 2 Question-Response

31

1. Mark your answer. Ⓐ Ⓑ Ⓒ
2. Mark your answer. Ⓐ Ⓑ Ⓒ
3. Mark your answer. Ⓐ Ⓑ Ⓒ

Part 3 Conversation

32

1. What is Beatles Fest?
   (A) It's a film festival.
   (B) It's a religious festival.
   (C) It's a music festival.
   (D) It's a food festival.

   Ⓐ Ⓑ Ⓒ Ⓓ

2. Where is the festival?
   (A) In Tokyo
   (B) In New York
   (C) In Paris
   (D) In London

   Ⓐ Ⓑ Ⓒ Ⓓ

3. When will the man and woman go to Beatles Fest?
   (A) April 1st
   (B) April 2nd
   (C) April 3rd
   (D) They won't go.

   Ⓐ Ⓑ Ⓒ Ⓓ

Part 4 Talk

33

1. In which year did the Beatles visit America?
   (A) In 1963
   (B) In 1964
   (C) In 1965
   (D) In 1966

   Ⓐ Ⓑ Ⓒ Ⓓ

2. What TV show did the Beatles appear on?
   (A) The Johnny Carson Show
   (B) The Andy Griffith Show
   (C) The Ed Sullivan Show
   (D) The Jay Leno Show

   Ⓐ Ⓑ Ⓒ Ⓓ

3. How many people watched the show?
   (A) 73,000
   (B) 730,000
   (C) 7,300,000
   (D) 73,000,000

   Ⓐ Ⓑ Ⓒ Ⓓ

Unit 9 Art Museum 美術館

Before Listening

Match the words.

1. displayed	(A) skill
2. technique	(B) well-known
3. famous	(C) connected to the Internet
4. online	(D) exhibited

Part 1 Photograph

34

Ⓐ Ⓑ Ⓒ Ⓓ

Part 2 Question-Response

35

1. Mark your answer. Ⓐ Ⓑ Ⓒ
2. Mark your answer. Ⓐ Ⓑ Ⓒ
3. Mark your answer. Ⓐ Ⓑ Ⓒ

Part 3 Conversation

36

1. What is the National Gallery?
   (A) It's an art museum.
   (B) It's a natural history museum.
   (C) It's a war museum.
   (D) It's a science museum.
   Ⓐ Ⓑ Ⓒ Ⓓ

2. How much does it cost to enter the National Gallery?
   (A) 5 pounds
   (B) 10 pounds
   (C) 15 pounds
   (D) Nothing, it's free.
   Ⓐ Ⓑ Ⓒ Ⓓ

3. Which underground train station is near the National Gallery?
   (A) Charing Cross
   (B) Waterloo
   (C) Victoria
   (D) Piccadilly
   Ⓐ Ⓑ Ⓒ Ⓓ

Part 4 Talk

37

1. How many artists have paintings displayed at the Summerfield Art Gallery?
   (A) 1
   (B) 2
   (C) 3
   (D) 4
   Ⓐ Ⓑ Ⓒ Ⓓ

2. What does the guide say about Oscar Darver?
   (A) He was famous.
   (B) He is alive today.
   (C) Nobody knew about him.
   (D) He is from Russia.
   Ⓐ Ⓑ Ⓒ Ⓓ

3. What's special about the tour?
   (A) It's cheap to enter.
   (B) It features mainly sculptures.
   (C) It is online.
   (D) Visitors can meet the artists.
   Ⓐ Ⓑ Ⓒ Ⓓ

Unit 10 Sightseeing 観光

Before Listening

Fill in the blanks with correct words.

1. The garden is open to the public on weekdays.
   = The garden is open to the public from (　　　　　　) to Friday.
2. We will have a rest before the lesson.
   = We will have a (　　　　　　) before the lesson.
3. Let's take a picture together.
   = Let's take a (　　　　　　) together.

Part 1 Photograph

38

(A) (B) (C) (D)

Part 2 Question-Response

39

1. Mark your answer. (A) (B) (C)
2. Mark your answer. (A) (B) (C)
3. Mark your answer. (A) (B) (C)

Part 3 Conversation

40

1. What does the woman want to do?
   (A) Go shopping
   (B) Do some exercise
   (C) Go sightseeing
   (D) Do some gardening

   Ⓐ Ⓑ Ⓒ Ⓓ

2. When can tourists visit the royal palace?
   (A) Anytime on weekends
   (B) On weekday mornings
   (C) On weekday afternoons
   (D) On weekday evenings

   Ⓐ Ⓑ Ⓒ Ⓓ

3. Where does the woman want to go?
   (A) To a shopping mall
   (B) To a department store
   (C) To a lovely garden
   (D) To the gym

   Ⓐ Ⓑ Ⓒ Ⓓ

Part 4 Talk

41

1. Who is the speaker talking to?
   (A) A group of tourists
   (B) A group of students
   (C) The President of the United States of America
   (D) A group of journalists

   Ⓐ Ⓑ Ⓒ Ⓓ

2. What will they see in the morning?
   (A) The Washington Monument
   (B) The Vietnam Veterans Memorial
   (C) The Constitution Gardens
   (D) The White House

   Ⓐ Ⓑ Ⓒ Ⓓ

3. What's the last thing they will see today?
   (A) The Washington Monument
   (B) The White House
   (C) The Constitution Gardens
   (D) The Lincoln Memorial

   Ⓐ Ⓑ Ⓒ Ⓓ

Unit 11 Castles 城

Before Listening

Which sentence is NOT correct?

1. (A) The castle looks interesting.
   (B) The castle looks like interesting.
2. (A) The castle looks a white bird.
   (B) The castle looks like a white bird.
3. (A) The Secret Garden sounds romantic.
   (B) The Secret Garden sounds like romantic.

Part 1 Photograph

42

Ⓐ Ⓑ Ⓒ Ⓓ

Part 2 Question-Response

43

1. Mark your answer. Ⓐ Ⓑ Ⓒ
2. Mark your answer. Ⓐ Ⓑ Ⓒ
3. Mark your answer. Ⓐ Ⓑ Ⓒ

Part 3 Conversation

44

1. When will the couple visit the castle?
   (A) On Thursday
   (B) On Friday
   (C) On Saturday
   (D) On Sunday
   Ⓐ Ⓑ Ⓒ Ⓓ

2. What will they do at the castle?
   (A) visit the gardens
   (B) enter the castle building
   (C) go on a guided tour
   (D) play with the animals
   Ⓐ Ⓑ Ⓒ Ⓓ

3. How much will the tickets cost?
   (A) They are free.
   (B) 10 pounds
   (C) 20 pounds
   (D) 30 pounds
   Ⓐ Ⓑ Ⓒ Ⓓ

Part 4 Talk

45

1. Who is talking?
   (A) A tourist
   (B) A history teacher
   (C) A tour guide
   (D) A police officer
   Ⓐ Ⓑ Ⓒ Ⓓ

2. When was the castle built?
   (A) in 1264
   (B) in 1462
   (C) in 1749
   (D) in 1947
   Ⓐ Ⓑ Ⓒ Ⓓ

3. How many people have visited the castle since it opened to the public?
   (A) More than 1,000
   (B) More than 10,000
   (C) More than 100,000
   (D) More than 1,000,000
   Ⓐ Ⓑ Ⓒ Ⓓ

Unit 12 Halloween Festival ハロウィーン

Before Listening

Which sentence is NOT correct?

1. (A) Your Halloween costume is scary.
   (B) Your Halloween costume is scared.
2. (A) I'm interesting in the history of Halloween.
   (B) I'm interested in the history of Halloween.
3. (A) The Halloween party was boring.
   (B) The Halloween party was bored.

Part 1 Photograph

46

Ⓐ Ⓑ Ⓒ Ⓓ

Part 2 Question-Response

47

1. Mark your answer. Ⓐ Ⓑ Ⓒ
2. Mark your answer. Ⓐ Ⓑ Ⓒ
3. Mark your answer. Ⓐ Ⓑ Ⓒ

Part 3 Conversation

48

1. Who is the boy talking to?
   (A) His teacher
   (B) His mother
   (C) His sister
   (D) His friend
   Ⓐ Ⓑ Ⓒ Ⓓ

2. What will the boy dress up as for the Halloween party?
   (A) A ghost
   (B) A zombie
   (C) A monster
   (D) A scarecrow
   Ⓐ Ⓑ Ⓒ Ⓓ

3. Why won't the boy go trick or treating this year?
   (A) Because his costume is too scary
   (B) Because he has no money
   (C) Because his parents don't want him to go
   (D) Because he thinks he is too old
   Ⓐ Ⓑ Ⓒ Ⓓ

Part 4 Talk

49

1. When is Halloween?
   (A) October 1st
   (B) October 13th
   (C) October 23rd
   (D) October 31st
   Ⓐ Ⓑ Ⓒ Ⓓ

2. What happens in some schools in the US or Canada on Halloween?
   (A) The schools have a day off.
   (B) The teachers give the kids candy.
   (C) The schools have Halloween parties.
   (D) The schools have special Halloween lessons.
   Ⓐ Ⓑ Ⓒ Ⓓ

3. When do children usually go trick-or-treating?
   (A) In the morning
   (B) At lunchtime
   (C) In the afternoon
   (D) In the evening
   Ⓐ Ⓑ Ⓒ Ⓓ

Unit 13 Fashion ファッション

Before Listening

Choose the best words to complete the sentences.

1. In this shop, I'm looking (　　　) a jacket.
   (A) with　　(B) to　　(C) for
2. The sleeves are (　　　) short for me.
   (A) to　　(B) too　　(C) till
3. Your shoes (　　　) the color of your skin.
   (A) match　　(B) look　　(C) appear
4. They gave good advice about (　　　) to look taller.
   (A) what　　(B) which　　(C) how

Part 1 Photograph

50

Ⓐ Ⓑ Ⓒ Ⓓ

Part 2 Question-Response

51

1. Mark your answer.　Ⓐ Ⓑ Ⓒ
2. Mark your answer.　Ⓐ Ⓑ Ⓒ
3. Mark your answer.　Ⓐ Ⓑ Ⓒ

Part 3 Conversation

52

1. What item of clothing are they talking about?
   (A) A pair of trousers
   (B) A pair of shorts
   (C) A jacket
   (D) A hat
   Ⓐ Ⓑ Ⓒ Ⓓ

2. What is the problem?
   (A) It's the wrong color.
   (B) It's the wrong style.
   (C) It's the wrong size.
   (D) It's too expensive.
   Ⓐ Ⓑ Ⓒ Ⓓ

3. How much does it cost?
   (A) 100 pounds
   (B) 150 pounds
   (C) 200 pounds
   (D) 250 pounds
   Ⓐ Ⓑ Ⓒ Ⓓ

Part 4 Talk

53

1. Who is speaking?
   (A) A school teacher
   (B) A shop assistant
   (C) A customer
   (D) A YouTuber
   Ⓐ Ⓑ Ⓒ Ⓓ

2. What does the speaker give advice about?
   (A) How to look younger
   (B) How to look slimmer
   (C) How to look taller
   (D) How to be more confident
   Ⓐ Ⓑ Ⓒ Ⓓ

3. What does the speaker advise for people who want to look more fashionable?
   (A) To wear an accessory
   (B) To wear formal clothes
   (C) To wear clothes in simple colors
   (D) To wear tight-fitting clothes
   Ⓐ Ⓑ Ⓒ Ⓓ

Unit 14 Library 図書館にて

Before Listening

Choose the best words to complete the sentences.

1. The library is open at nine (　　) the morning.
   (A) at　(B) for　(C) in
2. You can borrow the book (　　) two weeks.
   (A) at　(B) for　(C) to
3. The library card is free (　　) charge.
   (A) at　(B) of　(C) by
4. Fiction books are (　　) the second floor.
   (A) on　(B) for　(C) in

Part 1 Photograph

54

Ⓐ Ⓑ Ⓒ Ⓓ

Part 2 Question-Response

55

1. Mark your answer.　Ⓐ Ⓑ Ⓒ
2. Mark your answer.　Ⓐ Ⓑ Ⓒ
3. Mark your answer.　Ⓐ Ⓑ Ⓒ

Part 3 Conversation

56

1. Where is the conversation taking place?
   (A) At a library
   (B) At a bookstore
   (C) At a cafe
   (D) At a school
   Ⓐ Ⓑ Ⓒ Ⓓ

2. What does the woman want to do?
   (A) Borrow a book
   (B) Browse the books
   (C) Buy a book
   (D) Study
   Ⓐ Ⓑ Ⓒ Ⓓ

3. Which of the following is a benefit of getting a library card?
   (A) You can buy books cheaply.
   (B) Library cards are inexpensive.
   (C) You can borrow books for longer.
   (D) You can borrow more books.
   Ⓐ Ⓑ Ⓒ Ⓓ

Part 4 Talk

57

1. Who is speaking?
   (A) A librarian
   (B) A teacher
   (C) A customer
   (D) A visitor to a library
   Ⓐ Ⓑ Ⓒ Ⓓ

2. On which date is the library closed?
   (A) Monday, January 1st
   (B) Monday, May 23rd
   (C) Sunday, July 17th
   (D) Sunday, October 2nd
   Ⓐ Ⓑ Ⓒ Ⓓ

3. On which floor can you find fiction books?
   (A) 1st
   (B) 2nd
   (C) 3rd
   (D) 4th
   Ⓐ Ⓑ Ⓒ Ⓓ

Unit 15 Harry Potter ハリー・ポッター

Before Listening

Select the appropriate sentences.

1. (A) Have you reading all the Harry Potter books?
   (B) Have you read all the Harry Potter books?
2. (A) Which do you prefer the books or the movies?
   (B) Which do you prefer the books and the movies?
3. (A) J.K. Rowling loved to read.
   (B) J.K. Rowling loved to reading.
4. (A) She married by the man.
   (B) She married the man.

Part 1 Photograph

58

Ⓐ Ⓑ Ⓒ Ⓓ

Part 2 Question-Response

59

1. Mark your answer. Ⓐ Ⓑ Ⓒ
2. Mark your answer. Ⓐ Ⓑ Ⓒ
3. Mark your answer. Ⓐ Ⓑ Ⓒ

Part 3 Conversation

60

1. Which is the woman's favorite Harry Potter movie?
   (A) *Philosopher's Stone*
   (B) *Chamber of Secrets*
   (C) *Prisoner of Azkaban*
   (D) *Deathly Hallows* Ⓐ Ⓑ Ⓒ Ⓓ

2. Who is the man's favorite actor or actress in the movies?
   (A) Daniel Radcliffe
   (B) Emma Watson
   (C) Rupert Grint
   (D) Maggie Smith Ⓐ Ⓑ Ⓒ Ⓓ

3. Which do they like best, the books or the movies?
   (A) They both prefer the books.
   (B) They both prefer the movies.
   (C) The man prefers the books, the woman prefers the movies.
   (D) The woman prefers the books, the man prefers the movies. Ⓐ Ⓑ Ⓒ Ⓓ

Part 4 Talk

61

1. What was Joanne Rowling's job while she was living in Portugal?
   (A) A translator
   (B) A teacher
   (C) A writer
   (D) A journalist Ⓐ Ⓑ Ⓒ Ⓓ

2. What was the name of Joanne Rowling's first husband?
   (A) Neil Murray
   (B) Jessica Rowling
   (C) Jorge Arantes
   (D) Daniel Radcliffe Ⓐ Ⓑ Ⓒ Ⓓ

3. How many children does she have?
   (A) 0
   (B) 1
   (C) 2
   (D) 3 Ⓐ Ⓑ Ⓒ Ⓓ

Unit 16 Family 家族

Before Listening

Fill in the blanks to complete the sentences.

1. He is unemployed.
   = He is ( ) of work.
2. She loves reading.
   = She loves ( ) read.
3. He is my sibling.
   = He is my ( ).

Part 1 Photograph

62

(A) (B) (C) (D)

Part 2 Question-Response

63

1. Mark your answer. (A) (B) (C)
2. Mark your answer. (A) (B) (C)
3. Mark your answer. (A) (B) (C)

Part 3 Conversation

64

1. How many brothers and sisters does the man have?
   (A) 2 brothers
   (B) 2 brothers and 1 sister
   (C) 2 sisters and 1 brother
   (D) 2 sisters

   Ⓐ Ⓑ Ⓒ Ⓓ

2. How old is the man's eldest sibling?
   (A) 17 years old
   (B) 18 years old
   (C) 19 years old
   (D) 20 years old

   Ⓐ Ⓑ Ⓒ Ⓓ

3. Where does the family live?
   (A) In a house in the city
   (B) In an apartment in the city
   (C) In a house in the countryside
   (D) In an apartment in the countryside

   Ⓐ Ⓑ Ⓒ Ⓓ

Part 4 Talk

65

1. Who is Sam?
   (A) Maria's father
   (B) Maria's mother
   (C) Maria's sister
   (D) Maria's brother

   Ⓐ Ⓑ Ⓒ Ⓓ

2. What is Maria's hobby?
   (A) Watching YouTube
   (B) Doing maths puzzles
   (C) Reading books
   (D) Playing video games

   Ⓐ Ⓑ Ⓒ Ⓓ

3. What is James' job?
   (A) He is unemployed.
   (B) He is a banker.
   (C) He is an accountant.
   (D) He is a YouTuber.

   Ⓐ Ⓑ Ⓒ Ⓓ

Unit 17 Cooking 料理

Before Listening

Match the words.

1. recipe	(A) a piece of writing that says what something is like
2. description	(B) a set of instructions that tells you how to cook something
3. ingredient	(C) a skilled cook, especially the main cook in a restaurant or hotel
4. chef	(D) one of the foods that are used to make a dish

Part 1 Photograph

66

Ⓐ Ⓑ Ⓒ Ⓓ

Part 2 Question-Response

67

1. Mark your answer. Ⓐ Ⓑ Ⓒ
2. Mark your answer. Ⓐ Ⓑ Ⓒ
3. Mark your answer. Ⓐ Ⓑ Ⓒ

Part 3 Conversation

68

1. What is the man cooking for dinner?
   (A) Mushroom stroganoff
   (B) Mushroom omelet
   (C) Mushroom pizza
   (D) Mushroom soup

   Ⓐ Ⓑ Ⓒ Ⓓ

2. Where did he get the recipe?
   (A) From a TV program
   (B) From a cookbook
   (C) From a Russian friend
   (D) From the Internet

   Ⓐ Ⓑ Ⓒ Ⓓ

3. Which of the following is an ingredient in the dinner?
   (A) Chicken
   (B) Onions
   (C) Cheese
   (D) Eggplant

   Ⓐ Ⓑ Ⓒ Ⓓ

Part 4 Talk

69

1. Who is talking?
   (A) A YouTuber
   (B) A teacher in a cooking class
   (C) A TV chef
   (D) A mother to her children

   Ⓐ Ⓑ Ⓒ Ⓓ

2. Which ingredient is added at the end?
   (A) Mushrooms
   (B) Onions
   (C) Sour cream
   (D) Stock

   Ⓐ Ⓑ Ⓒ Ⓓ

3. What is the dish served with?
   (A) Potatoes
   (B) Bread
   (C) Rice
   (D) Salad

   Ⓐ Ⓑ Ⓒ Ⓓ

Unit 18 Advertisement 広告

Before Listening

Choose the best word to complete the sentence.

1. These words are related (　　) social media.
   (A) to　　(B) by　　(C) for
2. I'm not influenced (　　) advertisements.
   (A) at　　(B) by　　(C) for
3. The new vacuum cleaner is (　　) the market today.
   (A) with　　(B) on　　(C) by
4. The battery lasts (　　) 10 hours.
   (A) to　　(B) by　　(C) for

Part 1 Photograph

70

Ⓐ Ⓑ Ⓒ Ⓓ

Part 2 Question-Response

71

1. Mark your answer.　Ⓐ Ⓑ Ⓒ
2. Mark your answer.　Ⓐ Ⓑ Ⓒ
3. Mark your answer.　Ⓐ Ⓑ Ⓒ

Part 3 Conversation

72

1. What was the advertisement for?
   (A) A computer
   (B) Cold medicine
   (C) A TV
   (D) Clothes

   Ⓐ Ⓑ Ⓒ Ⓓ

2. How much did the company grow because of the advertisement?
   (A) 12%
   (B) 22%
   (C) 32%
   (D) 42%

   Ⓐ Ⓑ Ⓒ Ⓓ

3. What was the main point of the advertisement?
   (A) To tell people about a special discount price
   (B) To tell people about a company's success
   (C) To tell people about a product's quality
   (D) To tell people about a new service

   Ⓐ Ⓑ Ⓒ Ⓓ

Part 4 Talk

73

1. What is the name of the product that is being advertised?
   (A) Sucker NV10
   (B) Sucker NV20
   (C) Sucker NV30
   (D) Sucker NV40

   Ⓐ Ⓑ Ⓒ Ⓓ

2. What is a special feature of the vacuum cleaner?
   (A) It is very small and compact.
   (B) It cleans using water.
   (C) It has an extra-long power cable.
   (D) It has no bags.

   Ⓐ Ⓑ Ⓒ Ⓓ

3. How long does the rechargeable battery last?
   (A) 10 hours
   (B) 20 hours
   (C) 30 hours
   (D) 400 hours

   Ⓐ Ⓑ Ⓒ Ⓓ

Unit 19 COVID-19 新型コロナウイルス

Before Listening

Match the words.

1. emergency	(A) a thing that you must have and cannot live without
2. immediately	(B) at once
3. necessity	(C) a shop that sells medicines and drugs
4. pharmacy	(D) a serious and dangerous situation

Part 1 Photograph

74

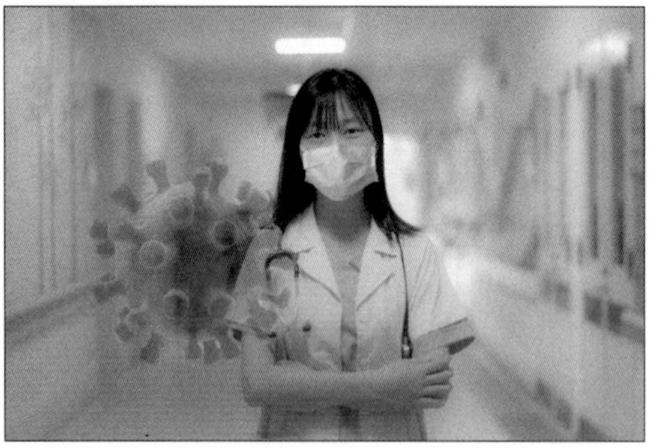

Ⓐ Ⓑ Ⓒ Ⓓ

Part 2 Question-Response

75

1. Mark your answer. Ⓐ Ⓑ Ⓒ
2. Mark your answer. Ⓐ Ⓑ Ⓒ
3. Mark your answer. Ⓐ Ⓑ Ⓒ

Part 3 Conversation

76

1. What are they talking about?
   (A) Getting vaccinated for Covid-19
   (B) A new variant of coronavirus
   (C) A new restaurant they want to visit
   (D) A new type of mask that prevents Covid-19 infection
   Ⓐ Ⓑ Ⓒ Ⓓ

2. How many people caught Covid-19 yesterday?
   (A) 30
   (B) 300
   (C) 3,000
   (D) 30,000
   Ⓐ Ⓑ Ⓒ Ⓓ

3. What will happen tomorrow?
   (A) They will buy some new masks.
   (B) They will visit a restaurant.
   (C) The shops will close.
   (D) Restaurants and bars will close.
   Ⓐ Ⓑ Ⓒ Ⓓ

Part 4 Talk

77

1. Who is speaking?
   (A) A patient in a hospital
   (B) A nurse
   (C) A leader of a country
   (D) A company boss
   Ⓐ Ⓑ Ⓒ Ⓓ

2. When do the new rules start?
   (A) This evening
   (B) Tomorrow morning
   (C) The weekend
   (D) Next week
   Ⓐ Ⓑ Ⓒ Ⓓ

3. What must people do when the new rules start?
   (A) Get vaccinated for coronavirus
   (B) Go back to work
   (C) Get tested for coronavirus
   (D) Stay at home
   Ⓐ Ⓑ Ⓒ Ⓓ

Unit 20 Celebrating Christmas クリスマス

Before Listening

Which sentence is correct?

1. (A) E-cards are more cheap than paper cards.
   (B) E-cards are cheaper than paper cards.
2. (A) I haven't decided already.
   (B) I haven't decided yet.
3. (A) They eat a special meal called 'Christmas dinner.'
   (B) They eat a special meal calling 'Christmas dinner.'
4. (A) Christmas is similar like New Year in Japan.
   (B) Christmas is similar to New Year in Japan.

Part 1 Photograph

78

Ⓐ Ⓑ Ⓒ Ⓓ

Part 2 Question-Response

79

1. Mark your answer. Ⓐ Ⓑ Ⓒ
2. Mark your answer. Ⓐ Ⓑ Ⓒ
3. Mark your answer. Ⓐ Ⓑ Ⓒ

Part 3 Conversation

80

1. What is Maria doing?
   (A) She is shopping for Christmas gifts.
   (B) She is going for a walk.
   (C) She is on a date with her boyfriend.
   (D) She is watching a Christmas movie.

   Ⓐ Ⓑ Ⓒ Ⓓ

2. Who is Maria going to buy a belt for?
   (A) Herself
   (B) Her boyfriend
   (C) Her mother
   (D) Her father

   Ⓐ Ⓑ Ⓒ Ⓓ

3. Who will do their Christmas shopping online?
   (A) John
   (B) Maria
   (C) Maria's boyfriend
   (D) Maria's mother

   Ⓐ Ⓑ Ⓒ Ⓓ

Part 4 Talk

81

1. How many national holidays are there for Christmas in the UK?
   (A) 1
   (B) 2
   (C) 3
   (D) 4

   Ⓐ Ⓑ Ⓒ Ⓓ

2. What do people eat for Christmas Dinner?
   (A) Chicken
   (B) Noodles
   (C) Fruit salad
   (D) Turkey

   Ⓐ Ⓑ Ⓒ Ⓓ

3. Which of the following does the speaker NOT say about Christmas in the UK?
   (A) Young couples go on dates.
   (B) There is a special meal.
   (C) People go to church.
   (D) People exchange gifts.

   Ⓐ Ⓑ Ⓒ Ⓓ

Happy
Holidays

著作権法上，無断複写・複製は禁じられています。

Easy Listening Practice for the New TOEIC® L&R Test

やさしいTOEIC® L&Rテスト　リスニングパート攻略　[B-969]

1　刷　2024年4月1日

著　者　バーデン・タイラー　Tyler Burden
千葉　剛　Tsuyoshi Chiba
鄭　耀星　Yau-Sin Cheng
深澤　清　Kiyoshi Fukasawa
福岡　賢昌　Takamasa Fukuoka
鷲谷　里美　Satomi Washiya

発行者　南雲一範　Kazunori Nagumo
発行所　株式会社　南雲堂
〒162-0801　東京都新宿区山吹町361
NAN'UN-DO Co., Ltd.
361 Yamabuki-cho, Shinjuku-ku, Tokyo 162-0801, Japan
振替口座：00160-0-46863
TEL: 03-3268-2311（営業部：学校関係）
03-3268-2384（営業部：書店関係）
03-3268-2387（編集部）
FAX: 03-3269-2486

編集者　加藤　敦
装　丁　Nスタジオ
組　版　Office haru
検　印　省　略
コード　ISBN978-4-523-17969-6　C0082

Printed in Japan

E-mail　nanundo@post.email.ne.jp
URL　https://www.nanun-do.co.jp/